Dedication

To Lane and Chris, two great sons God has blessed Norma and I with.   We see the start of them taking root in God.   Fruit will follow.

Copyright: Carlton L. Coon Sr.
              4521 North Farm Road 165
              Springfield, Missouri

All rights reserved.   Duplication of material in this book is not permitted without copyright holders permission.

All scriptures are from the KJV unless otherwise noted.

Acknowledgments

To those who have preceded me in providing material for newcomers in Christ: Loren Yadon, Crawford Coon, the late David Gray, and Jack Yonts.

Those who have taken the responsibility for teaching this material to newcomers that I have had the privilege of pastoring are Lee Suttles, our first New Convert Care Director, now starting a Home Missions church, Curt Reavis who also taught the material, (Curt and his wife Ruby are also now launching a new church), my dear wife Norma, who now takes care of feeding the new lambs; and of course Mike Textor and Pam Bagley, who have most recently taught this material.

Editing - Norma Coon, Jeanette Moore, David Black, Diane Rose, Mike Textor, Hannah Textor, and Lee Smith

Truth Publication's ministry team - Linda Gold and Norma Coon

Office Staff who assisted in bringing this material into this format - Diane Rose, Hannah Textor, Norma Coon, and Linda Gold.

A church full of great people that I had the privilege to pastor in Springfield, Missouri. Truth Tabernacle's legacy of impacting the world will remain regardless! Thanks for your support and encouragement.

About the Author

Take Root was developed while Carlton L. Coon Sr. pastored Truth Tabernacle United Pentecostal Church in Springfield, Missouri. After this pastorate, he served as General Director of the Home Missions Division of the United Pentecostal Church, International He is married to the former Norma Terrell of Elmer, Louisiana. They have two sons - Lane married to Shelley Stewart and Chris. Three "holy children" (2 grandsons and a granddaughter) have been added - Kaden Christopher, Wyatt Lane and Elsie Adara.

The Coons also pastored the Vidalia Revival Center of Vidalia, Louisiana for over eight years. The church was a Home Missions church less than 18 months old when the Coons began their pastorate.

Coon is the author of nineteen books - including *The Daily Things of Christian Living* published in 1994, *New Convert Care* published in 1992, and *Follow Up Visitation* also published in 1992 and *If Everybody Here Were Just Like Me* in 2010. A complete list of books and resources as well as ordering information can be found in the back of this book.

Coon served as the initiating Chairman of the Vidalia Chamber of Commerce, on the Board of Directors of Gateway College of Evangelism, chaired the committee for the annual Men's Conference of the Missouri District of the United Pentecostal Church, presbyter on the Missouri District Board and as Secretary of the General Home Missions Division. The Coons have ministered at various meetings around the world.

Table of Contents

Introduction 11

Session One - "Welcome to the Church" 13
    Survey 17

Session Two - "Doctrinal Overview" 19
    Survey 23

Session Three - "How to Effectively Share Your Faith!" 25
    Survey 29

Session Four - "You and Your Pastor" 31
    Survey 35

Session Five - "Stewardship" 37
    Survey 41

Session Six - "Financial Stewardship - Tithing" 43
    Survey 47

Session Seven - "Financial Stewardship - Giving" 49
    Survey 53

Session Eight - "The Lifestyle of a Christian, Part I" 55
    Survey 61

Session Nine - "The Lifestyle of a Christian, Part II" 63
    Survey 67

Session Ten - "Specific Principles of Christian Living" 69
    Survey 79

Session Eleven - "Overcoming Temptation" 81
    Survey 85

Introduction to Teacher's Manual

The care of those who are new to Christ's body is an important work. One portion of discipleship is through teaching. The material in this book has eleven lessons designed for newcomers. In contrast to the first series of lessons, <u>Take Root</u>, for the most part, these lessons deal with our Christian responsibilities.

The purpose of this teacher's booklet is to acquaint you with how this material may best be used. It was originally developed for a classroom environment, but has also been used by students in independent studies.

The Importance of Focused Teaching of "Spiritual Babes"

In more than twelve years of pastoring, our two pastorates have not retained a single convert that could not find time to participate in a "Newcomer's Class." That is an amazing statistic. Our capacity to disciple the new believer is strengthened by a small class environment that allows time for questions and participation.

Instructions for teachers:

1. Many of these lessons have far more material than can be covered in a fifty minute session. For this reason, it is recommended that you not read all of the scriptures in each lesson. Select those that you feel present the material in the clearest light, and use these in your sessions.
2. Preparation is important. There may come a time when you can walk into the classroom and teach this material without a great amount of time spent in preparation. Initially, this will not be true. Expect to spend several hours each week getting ready for your class.
3. Keep attendance records. Attempt to get each student the material when they are absent.
4. Several lessons require the input of your pastor. As a matter of fact, he may choose to teach the lessons on Christian lifestyle. I have followed this practice for the past several years.

In the classroom:

1. Each student should be provided with the lesson material. The student's material is similar to the instructor's manual.
2. Keep the students as relaxed as possible. If your situation permits, having coffee or soda available seems to create a more comfortable environment.
3. Preferably, tables will be provided for students to place their handbooks on.
4. The instructors should orient themselves to guiding the sessions in a discussion type format. This is a more informal approach that provides greater opportunities for questions.
5. Have students do the scripture reading in class. During the first session, ask

the class if anyone does not wish to read. *Be sure not to call on those who indicate they would rather not read.*

6. Each student handbook has material that the student should study at home and then return to their instructor at the next class session. After reviewing each student's material, the instructor should return the material as soon as possible.

Honoring the graduates:

After the students have completed the lesson material, it is important to give them full recognition. It has proved successful to have graduations that honor those students who have completed their lesson material. For the first time, some of these people have actually completed something that required extra effort on their part. They deserve to be recognized. Diplomas that certify having completed at least 80% of the homework are given out at this graduation. For those who did not meet this criteria, provide a certificate of attendance. Have a number of people prepared to lead "spontaneous" applause, accompanied by whistles, cheers, etc. during this Sunday celebration.

This material is the result of over ten years of "hands-on" usage. As is always true, nothing is created in a vacuum. A number of previous publications influenced the production of this material. Loren Yadon's, From an Acorn to an Oak, and Crawford Coon's, Christian Development Publications, are most noteworthy.

> ## Session One
> ### WELCOME TO THE CHURCH
> **Goal of This Lesson:** This lesson gives the focus of the local church. Every church must have a vision and an understood mission. The more often this can be communicated, the more effective the church will be in accomplishing its goals.

Note to teacher: The pastor can help you better understand the goals and methods of the local church. His understanding of God's vision for the congregation needs to be communicated. Be sure to inject this local information into the lesson. For this lesson, a supplemental handout could be developed to accompany the student handbook.

I. Let's define the church.

    A. Discuss: What is the Church? (*Note to teacher:* Allow time for discussion and student input before providing the Bible answer. Answers will likely include: a building, a group of people, a denomination, or a religious institution. Explain that the Greek word for church, *ekklesia* means, "a body of called out ones.")

    B. Discuss: What is the purpose for the existence of the church? *(Giving glory to God by the expansion of the kingdom of God. This is done through evangelizing and discipleship.)*

II. Discuss: What are the characteristics of a strong church?

    A. Matthew 16:16-18 (*Note to Teacher:* Read or have a student read aloud each of the scriptures.) contains the first usage of the term *church* in the New Testament. In these verses, Jesus describes a very dynamic organism rather than an organization. From what Jesus told Simon Peter we are able to understand:
       1. The church is (being built). This is an ongoing process. It is constantly being built. One writer said, "When we stop growing, we start dying." When churches or individual Christians reach a point that they think they have no further need for growth, it should be a danger sign. You must never stop growing in God!
       2. The church has a God given revelation of who Jesus is. "Thou art the Christ, the son of the living God."
       3. The church shall not be prevailed upon by the gates of hell. The *gates* as used here speak of the seat of influence or power

in a city. In referring to the *gates of hell*, Jesus refers to the most powerful influences that Satan and hell can offer. Notice the *gates of hell* are mentioned, not the gates of the church. It indicates the church is on the offensive rather than on the defensive.
4. Strong churches take the offensive against hell. Their objective is the expansion of the kingdom of God and the destruction of Satan's kingdom. This is done through constant evangelism and discipleship efforts.

➢ **Great churches are constantly being built, have a revelation of who Jesus is, and minister at the very strongholds of hell.**

B. Acts 2:41-46 (Read) gives some important characteristics of the early New Testament church. (*Note to Teacher:* The words and phrases that are in parentheses are blank in the student manual. Be sure to give your students time to fill in the blanks.)
 1. (Unity) of purpose
 2. They (fellowship) with one another
 3. Celebrate communion together.
 4. Prayer is an ongoing effort.
 5. The (apostle's doctrine), a solid set of teachings, are being provided.

➢ **Great churches are unified and have good fellowship. They keep Christ's death before them in communion. In great churches prayer is a priority, and they are doctrinally solid.**

C. A great church is like Antioch -   Acts 11:25-30 (Read)
 1. It opens its doors to those (unacceptable to others). Paul, as a new convert, frightened those who were already in the church.
 2. There were (spiritual leaders) other than the pastor.
 3. It sends (preachers) into the gospel work.

➢ **Great churches open themselves to those unacceptable to others. Great churches are measured by their sending capacity, not their seating capacity. Finally, great churches develop leaders.**

D. 1 Corinthians 14:12 (Read)   We are instructed to covet (spiritual gifts).

➢ **Great churches seek to excel. Nothing is done half-way. If something is worth doing, it is worth doing well.**

E. Philippians 4:10-23 (Read)

> **Great churches give liberally.**

III. Everything that excels, exists with a sense of purpose or a mission. Write down five things that define what you perceive to be the mission of our church.

1. _____
2. _____
3. _____
4. _____
5. _____

IV. Great churches are made up of great saints. Discuss: What makes a great saint? *(One who does the Lord's will)*

V. The power of commitment. In your mind, is it . . . *the* church, *their* church, *my* church, or *our* church? Committed people find themselves somewhere between the latter two - my church or our church.

    A. If it is your church, you have a responsibility of helping to fulfill its mission.

    B. If you were the pastor, what would you change to improve our church?

    C. What ministry opportunities do you see that we are not fulfilling?
    _____
    _____

VI. The Pastor's Vision for the church. *(Note to Teacher:* This material is not in the student manual. Please substitute material that your pastor provides.*)*

    A. (80%) of those attending involved in a definable ministry.

    B. (10%) of the membership of our church actively involved in organized evangelism. Organized evangelism is defined as Home Bible Studies, Follow-up Visitation, Bus Ministry, and Child Evangelism.

    C. (10%) of our people involved in intense spiritual warfare through (prayer).

**"If everyone in this church
were just like me,
what kind of church
would this church be?"**

Carlton L. Coon Sr. Bear Fruit – Teacher's Manual

Session One - Survey Sheet
"Welcome to the Church"

Name: _____ Date: _____

1. What is the church?

2. What does it mean when Matthew 16:18 says, ". . . and the gates of hell shall not prevail against it?"

3. Why do you suppose fellowship is an important characteristic of a great church?

4. Why do you suppose the believers in Jerusalem were afraid of Paul? How does that relate to our experience with new comers to our church?

5. Now that you have had more time to think about the question; what would you do to improve our church?

6. How do you see yourself making this a better church?

7. Is there any part of this lesson you would like to have more thoroughly explained?

> ## Session Two
> ### DOCTRINAL OVERVIEW: "WHAT MUST I DO TO BE SAVED?"
> **Goal of This Lesson:** To answer the following questions:
> - *What are the steps by which one is saved from his sin?*
> - *What is an individual responsible for?*
> - *What has God already done?*
> - *If God has already provided salvation, why must I do anything?*

Note to Teacher: If all of your students have completed *Take Root*, level one of this study, this lesson could possibly be excluded. We always include this for the sake of those who may have relocated from another church body. This lesson affirms the doctrinal position of the Bible and of our church.

I. Salvation begins with an awareness of one's sinfulness. Discuss: What are some of today's approaches to dealing with wrong? (Wrong is called "a mistake," "a disease," etc. - anything but sin.) In 1973, Psychologist Karl Meninger wrote a book asking the question, *Whatever Happened to Sin?* Meninger believed that we are part of a society that no longer is willing to be responsible for anything that occurs. Discuss: Why is there an aversion to calling something sin?

   A. What does the Bible say about our condition? (*Note to Teacher:* Have someone read the following verses aloud.)
      1. Romans 3:10 - There is (none) righteous . . .
      2. Romans 3:23 - All have (sinned) . . .

   B. Discuss: Based on the above verses of scripture, what is God's position on the goodness of man?

II. The Sin Problem - The Bible is clear - we are sinners; every one of us. As you look around this room, we have one thing in common; we are members of *Sinners Anonymous*. This leaves humanity in a dilemma: We are sinners. God is angry with the wicked every day. (Psalms 7:11) If we are to escape the wrath of an angry God, we must be saved.

III. An answer is provided - (*Note to Teacher:* The words and phrases that are in parentheses are blank in the student manual. Be sure to give your students time to fill in the blanks.) God has provided the possibility of salvation through the (Gospel). The word gospel basically means (good

<u>news)</u>. Now that we realize our sinfulness, we can understand why the gospel really is such good news.

    A. Discuss: What does the gospel consist of? (Have someone read the following verses.)

    B. 1 Corinthians 15:1-4 The good news is the <u>(death, burial, and resurrection of Jesus Christ)</u>.

    C. Romans 1:16 Further, the gospel is a powerful thing bringing us to salvation. The Greek word translated "power" is a word from which we get our English word *dynamite*. Suffice it to say, the gospel is powerful.

Without the gospel, there could be no salvation experience!

IV. There are two essential elements that God has made available to us. These are <u>(grace)</u> and <u>(faith)</u>. Discuss: Grace (Greek *charis*), the unmerited favor of God, a gift given with no expectation of a return on the investment. (Have someone read the following verses.)

    A. Ephesians 2:8 Discuss: In the verse, what things are gifts from God? (Grace is a gift, and the faith we are saved through is also a gift of God.)

    B. John 3:16 - We must believe, but according to Ephesians 2:8, the very fact that we can believe is a gift of God.

    C. Hebrews 11:6 - He that cometh must believe. The very capacity to believe is something God has provided us with.

V. *Discuss:* How your students define faith. Faith is more than a mental awareness. Faith takes action. It **does** something.

    A. (*Note to Teacher:* Give your students some time for the next exercise.) Write John 7:37-39 in your own words. (Space is provided in the student manual.)

    _____

    _____

    _____

    B. Discuss: How did you translate the portion that says, "... *believeth on me as the scripture hath said...*"? It seems that one can believe and *not* believe as the scripture hath said. While Jesus is teaching about the wonderful gift of the Holy Ghost that will come to believers, he acknowledges that it is possible to believe and not believe as the scripture says. In James 2:19 devils are shown as believing in one God and trembling. Obviously this believing does not make them saved. One can believe, and still be lost!

Faith is obedience in action.

Note to teacher: At this point, discuss the difference between the gospel and the plan of salvation. The gospel is the death, burial, and resurrection of Jesus Christ. However, just because there is good news does not mean one is saved. One can own a life preserver, but still drown because he doesn't have it on. The plan by which we are saved is discovered in the book of Acts where Simon Peter preaches the gospel which brings the people to the question, "What must we do?" Peter then provides them with the plan God has provided! A plan is available, but unless we obey the plan, we can still be lost.

VI. The Plan of Salvation - (Read Acts 2:38)

    A. Repentance - Have the students read the following.
        1. Matthew 4:17
        2. Acts 17:30
        3. Discuss: What is repentance? (A U-turn, an about-face, etc.)

    B. Baptism in Jesus Name. The word baptism comes from the Greek word "baptizo." *Baptizo* was used in the dyer's industry to speak of immersing a piece of cloth in dye. Scriptural baptism is by immersion. Read the following verses.
        1. Acts 10:44-48
        2. Acts 19:1-6
        3. Acts 8:16

    C. The final part of one's salvation experience is the promised infilling of the Holy Ghost. Among the verses that promise this experience:
        1. Joel 2:28-29
        2. John 7:37-39
        3. John 14:16-18

    D. In scriptural history the Holy Ghost always came with the initial evidence of speaking in other tongues. Read the following verses to validate this. At no time in the experience of the early church is

anyone shown receiving the Holy Ghost without there being a physical manifestation.
   1. Acts 2:1-4
   2. Acts 10:44-48
   3. Acts 19:1-6
   4. Please note that this is the initial experience with God. As we continue in our Christian life, we produce fruit of the spirit.

VII. Salvation consists of several things. One WAS saved from sin, IS experiencing salvation through the ongoing process of sanctification, and SHALL BE saved from eternal death and damnation. We always have something to praise God for if we have experienced the salvation he has so wonderfully provided.

Carlton L. Coon Sr.   *Bear Fruit – Teacher's Manual*

Session Two - Survey Sheet
"Doctrinal Overview"

Name: _____ Date: _____

1. Write out Romans 3:10 in your own words.

2. What does the word "gospel" mean? What is the gospel?

3. Ephesians 2:8-9 tells you what about your salvation? What has God provided so you can be saved?

4. How can one believe and still be lost?

5. What does it mean "to believe as the scripture hath said?"

6. What is repentance? How does one know they have truly repented?

7. What was the initial evidence of the Holy Ghost coming into Cornelius life?

8. Is there any part of this lesson you would like to have explained more completely?

Session Three
HOW TO EFFECTIVELY SHARE YOUR FAITH!

Goal of This Lesson: To introduce your students to various ways to share their faith. This is one of those times when the teacher needs to challenge the students to use the material in the coming week.

Note to Teacher: This lesson is the first in the material that focuses on the responsibilities of Christian living. It is helpful for the teacher to be involved in some form of evangelistic effort. If the directors of various outreaches (Bus Ministry, Home Bible Study, Children's Ministry, Follow Up Visitation, etc.) are available to discuss their ministry and vision for that ministry it can be helpful at getting the newcomer involved in some form of outreach.

I. Discuss: What is the highest purpose of God's Kingdom? (A very succinct answer to this question - evangelize the lost and disciple them, thus expanding the kingdom of God.)

II. There are many misconceptions about having a soul-winning ministry in God's Kingdom. Often, one who is untrained in outreach makes mistakes that work to the detriment of God's Kingdom, rather than to its advance. (*Note to teacher:* Take time to discuss each of these mistakes. Some of your students will have already been guilty of some of these things.)
We will discuss four common errors:

    A. Error #1 - Being too aggressive. One's friends and family are not usually won by telling them how wrong they are. One's approach should be filled with wisdom. In other words: Use common sense! Proverbs 11:30 - He that winneth souls is (wise).

    B. Error #2 - Fearfulness and timidity. Everyone needs and wants what you have experienced. Perhaps they do not yet know they need it. Our fear of sharing our faith is overcome by being involved in some area of that ministry.
       1. Read 2 Timothy 1:7. God hath not given us the spirit of (fear).
       2. Fear is overcome by training and application.

    C. Error #3 - Misconception of what a witness is. A witness tells what he or she knows. One may not know everything, but can witness about his or her own experience. In John 4, the Samaritan woman was not a theologian, but she was a great witness. The community came to meet Christ on the basis of her testimony.

D. Error #4 - Lack of knowledge or resources. There are times when one will be asked questions that should be answered in an effective and knowledgeable way.
   1. This can only be done through personal application.
   2. 1 Peter 3:15 - Encourages one to be ready to answer questions. There is nothing wrong with not having an answer the first time someone asks a given question, but you should never be caught without the answer a second time.

III. A Bible example of sharing one's experience is seen in the story of Andrew - John 1:35 - 42

   A. Andrew followed Jesus.

   B. Andrew found Peter, his brother.

   C. Peter and Andrew fellowshipped with Jesus.

IV. Six things can help us be successful soulwinners.

   A. Definite power - Pray for God's leadership and help in spreading your testimony. Prayer should be part of your constant effort of personal outreach. Holy Ghost power precedes witnessing power!

   B. Definite time to go - Lifestyle evangelism is the most powerful type of outreach. However, most of us need a concentrated time to go out into evangelistic efforts. Each church should have a time set aside that calls the congregation to evangelistic efforts. (*Note to Teacher*: Encourage your students to meet you at the next appointed visitation and outreach time. Your example will go far towards your students becoming participants in spreading the gospel.)

   C. Definite love to show to a definite project
      1. "God so loved the world . . ." has to be translated into "God so loved my next door neighbor, Barry!"
      2. Effective soul winners can always identify a particular person they are reaching with the gospel.

   D. Definite seed to sow
      1. What are you going to communicate?
      2. How do you plan to communicate it?
      3. People who succeed in evangelism can answer both of these questions.

E. Definite plan to know
   1. Memorize your testimony.
   2. Memorize a pattern for showing people the Bible premise for your experience with God. Initially, this can be marked in your Bible as a chain of linked references.
   3. The next pages of the lesson are given to provide a definite plan.

F. Definite follow through to growth. This is where we often fail. Just because you witness to an individual one time, does not remove your responsibilities. If we effectively follow-up on those we contact, there will be much greater results.

V. Definite plans for the student to know

   A. Have your students write out their personal testimony detailing how they came to God. Room is provided in the student handbook for this. Some of them may be good candidates for a "This is My Story" type testimonial to put in print. These can be powerful messages to those who receive them.

   B. Be aware of every outreach effort of the church. A certain area of ministry may fit one's personality perfectly, while in some other role one may be ineffective. Some such possibilities:
      1. Home Bible Study - Show the students a chart and explain its effectiveness.
      2. Bus Ministry - Introduce them to this ministry and its affect on the lives of children and families.
      3. Follow-Up-Visitation
      4. Telephone Follow-Up
      5. Divorce Recovery Ministry
      6. Jail and Prison Ministry
      7. Campus Ministry
      8. And so on, depending on the local church's efforts.

   C. Provide your students with patterns, like the one following, that can easily explain the gospel.

The Road to Salvation

Read: Romans 3:23
Explain: We all think, say, and do evil because of our sinful nature. Sin is simply anything that separates us from a pure and holy God. I can think of some things I have done that I know are wrong . . . can't you?

Read: Romans 6:23
Explain: As we receive wages on our job for what we do, so shall we receive wages for sin: Death - separation from God in this life and the hereafter. (See Revelations 20:12-15 - where the second death is spoken of.)

Read: Romans 5:8
Explain: Christ died for us . . . in our place. It is as if we were sentenced to death for a crime we committed and an innocent man offered to take our place. Our salvation is a possibility since Christ died in our stead.

Read: Acts 2:36 - 38
Explain: When the people Peter was speaking to realized Jesus Christ was Lord and died for them, they felt sorry for their sins and asked Peter what to do. First, he said, "repent" - turn from sin to God. *(Note to teacher: Now comes the hard part for many of us - closing the sale. Communicate to your students that they can lead someone to repentance while they are on a coffee-break at work.)* (Name of the person being witnessed to), do you believe that Jesus is Lord and He died for you? I feel sorry for my sins when I think of Calvary . . . don't you? Are you willing to give control of your life to God? Would you like to right now? (In your prayer, review each scripture. It is good to take the hand of the person you are praying with. Quite often they do not know how to pray. Your prayer will guide them.)

Read: Matthew 16:19
Explain: After asking for their important decision and praying with them, ask if they have repented. If they say, "yes," explain, "This is only the first step in the plan of salvation. Now you should be baptized in Jesus Name and receive the Holy Ghost!" (Review Acts 2:38 again.)

(*Note to Students:* It is not uncommon for people to say "No" when given an opportunity to repent. This is no cause for a feeling of rejection on your part. Simply say, "I understand your feelings and respect your decision. If you ever decide to give your life to Jesus, you know He loves you and can be found through repentance, baptism, and receiving the Holy Ghost." This response releases the pressure and leaves the door open for future discussions.)

Learning, memorizing, practicing, and using this method (or any variation of it you are comfortable with) will enable you to lead souls to Jesus.

Warning: Bringing people face to face with this truth is very powerful. Expect dramatic results!

Note to Teacher: You may want to give your students time to practice with each other.

Carlton L. Coon Sr. *Bear Fruit – Teacher's Manual*

Session Three - Survey Sheet
"How to Effectively Share Your Faith!"

Name: _____ Date: _____

1. How would a wise person witness to their friends and relatives?

2. What causes one to be afraid to share their faith? How can that fear be overcome?

3. What does a witness do?

4. Review John 1:35-42; what steps did Andrew take to cause his brother to choose to follow Christ?

5. Who do you want to see saved? This is a definite project. You can win that person by becoming an influence in their life.

6. Put *The Road to Salvation* in a chain reference in your Bible. Write the location of the next verse beside the first one you read and so on. Practice going through this with a friend.

7. Is there any part of this lesson you would like to have covered more thoroughly?

> ## Session Four
> ### YOU AND YOUR PASTOR
> **Goal of This Lesson:** To introduce the student to the ministerial 3office of their pastor. The role of the pastor in the development of the Christian life cannot be over emphasized. It is important to be comfortable with your spiritual leader and to recognize what his Biblical job description is. It is also essential to understand that we have responsibilities to our Pastor.

Note to Teacher: You have a responsibility to build up your pastor in the eyes of your students. This does not mean you are to make him into something he is not; but he is called of God to the spiritual leadership of the church. This calls for a special respect and honor.

I. God developed a unique approach in providing spiritual and physical leadership to his church. It is the role of a "pastor." Read Ephesians 4:11-15. *Discuss the various gifts God has given to the church: What is an apostle? a pastor/teacher? (Note: according to Greek scholar Kenneth Wuest, by virtue of the tenses used, the terms pastor and teacher refer to the same person) an evangelist? a prophet?* (Note to Teacher: Some of your student's perception of these things will be imperfect. Don't worry about correcting all of them. Remember the goal is to define the pastor's role.)

    A. There are six descriptive words in the New Testament relative to the Christian leadership and oversight of God's people:
        1. Shepherds - Acts 2:28
        2. Ensamples (examples) - 1 Peter 5:3
        3. Watchmen - Hebrews 13:17
        4. Rulers - 1 Timothy 5:17
        5. Pilots (translated governments in KJV) - 1 Corinthians 12:28
        6. Trustees of things committed to them - 2 Timothy 1:14, Titus 1:9

    B. Define Pastor: In the Greek New Testament a word meaning *shepherd* is translated pastor. So a pastor is a SHEPHERD of people! As the church, we are like a flock of sheep needing leadership.
        1. Discuss: What does a shepherd do? How do you suppose that could be applied to your pastor?

    C. What are the responsibilities of a pastor/shepherd? (Read Ezekiel

34:11-16).
1. Pastors are to (lead) the people.
2. Pastors (feed) the sheep.
3. Pastors (seek) the wandering.
4. Pastors (bind the broken).

D. (*Note to Teacher:* The following is an important point to make.) Some well meaning people attempt to put things in the pastor's job description that don't belong there. Some such things: legal advice, medical opinions, some aspects of financial advice, investment advice, even aspects of counseling. Pastors are not the church handy-man. While he may be willing to do such things, (Good leaders are always willing to be involved in doing the toughest jobs) relieve him as much as possible, of the responsibilities of mowing the grass, painting the sign, and such like. Furthermore, the pastor cannot be the only person in the church committed to outreach. It is important to support the pastor and allow him to fulfill the things God has called him to do.

E. Pastor/Teachers along with apostles, prophets, and evangelists are also to (mature) the saints for the (work of the ministry) (Read Ephesians 4:11-15).
1. Discuss: How does a pastor go about maturing the saints?
2. Discuss: What is the work of the ministry? (*Note to teacher:* Emphasize that all Christians are called to ministry. None of us are excluded. Ministry is simply service and servanthood.)

F. Pastors are commissioned to (preach) (Read 2 Timothy 4:2-5).

G. The pastor is a (watchman) to blow the trumpet and warn the people (Read Ezekiel 33:2-6).
1. Discuss: What would you want a watchman to warn you of? What form does the warning of a pastor take?

II. There are some things that pastors are not. Some of the items on this list are common sense, others are scriptural.

A. Lord over God's heritage. He is a leader, not a Lord. (1 Peter 5:1-4)

B. Your pastor is not without failings, nor is his wife and children.

C. He is not the pope. He is not infallible. His advice can misfire.

D. Pastors are not manipulators but motivators. The difference:

manipulators cause people to act for their own benefit and motivators do it for the common good.

E. Pastors do not misuse and abuse people.

F. Your pastor and his family are not plastic. They do hurt. Unkind statements and disappointments do affect them. They need your prayer, loyalty, and emotional support.

III. The qualifications of the ministry are found in (1 Timothy 3:1-13). Your pastor has met these qualifications:

A. Pastors are to be blameless. (verse 2) This means that no accusation could be made about his integrity. Nobody in the church or community can say he took advantage of them financially, or has been involved in sexual misconduct. Your pastor remains human, with human failings and human emotions, but he is a man of integrity.

B. His home-life must be in order. (verses 2, 4-5)

C. He must have self-discipline. (verse 3)

D. He must be spiritually mature, not a novice, having only recently come to Christ. (verse 6)

E. He must have a good report both with the church members and the community. (verse 7)

IV. There are a number of ways you can help your pastor.

A. Be (available) to develop your ministry and then to work in that ministry.

B. Be teachable - too many people come for the celebration but are not open to being taught the Word of God. Be present for every teaching session you can attend. Teaching is what matures your walk with God and gives you stability.

C. We should (respect) and (love) our spiritual leaders. (Read 1 Thessalonians 5:12-13).

D. As saints, we need to (live the gospel) (1 Corinthians 9:14). It is encouraging, when a pastor sees someone responding to what they are hearing.

E. Be an (encourager) of others and (attend church) (Hebrews 10:25).

F. (Pray) for and with the pastor (Romans 15:30). Your prayer for the pastor should include:
   1. His health - spiritually, mentally, emotionally, and physically.
   2. The pastor's family - Satan wants nothing more than to destroy a pastor's home and children. Give special prayer time for his children.
   3. That the pastor will have Godly wisdom.
   4. For Pastoral leadership.
   5. Divine anointing on the pastor as he preaches and teaches.

G. (Obey) them that rule over you for they watch for your souls (Read Hebrews 13:17, Romans 13:1-7). (*Note to Teacher:* If there is anything that deserves more attention, it is the subject of *submission* and *obedience*. In this age there is a "do our own thing" mentality. The greatest challenge for many new converts is the challenge of deciding to submit to the pastoral authority of their leader.)

H. Understand that your pastor is going to be required to give an eternal account for your submission or lack of the same.

V. Conclude the class with prayer for the pastor and his family. You will have to lead the prayer. Encourage your students to follow that example.

Carlton L. Coon Sr. *Bear Fruit – Teacher's Manual*

Session Four - Survey Sheet
"You and Your Pastor"

Name: _____ Date: _____

1. (This is not covered in the lesson; it will require some digging and thought on your part.) Ephesians 4:11-15 records some gifts God has provided the church. What are some other gifts God has made available to his church?

2. How do the six descriptive words used in speaking of Christian leadership apply to your expectations of the pastor? How is he a shepherd? How is he an example? How is he a watchman? How is he a ruler? How is he a pilot? How is he a trustee?

3. According to Ezekiel 34 a pastor is to do four things. What are they and how do they relate to your pastor?

4. How does the pastor prepare the saints for the work of the ministry?

5. What are some things you are willing to do to help your pastor?

6. Write Hebrews 13:17 in your own words.

7. Is there any part of this lesson you would like to have reviewed?

Session Five
STEWARDSHIP

Goal of This Lesson: Many people have no idea about the Christian approach to managing money. In this lesson, we want to make people aware of themselves as managers rather than owners.

Note to Teacher: This lesson contains more material than can be successfully covered in one forty-five minute session. This means extra work for you. However, it is important to condense and adjust in order to get in the principles on financial management.

Discussion: How many of you see some things around the church property that could be improved? What are some of those things? How do you suppose they are taken care of? What does it take to run your home? (Of course the answer is money. It takes money to operate a church.) Where does that money come from? (From the people who are part of the church.)

You see, all of the resources to advance the church have been made available to the church. Not only have they been made available to the church, but the provision has also been made through the saints. However, if the things God has provided are to get where they can help, the worshippers have to develop a rather unusual attitude toward life. In essence, we either become a conduit of blessing or a blessing limiter.

I. Several times the Bible uses a word that is not often part of our modern terminology. That term is *steward*. Discuss: (1) What is stewardship? (Management) (2) In what way is stewardship different than ownership? (3) Of what areas of life are we to be stewards?

II. Jesus' parable of Luke 19:12-27 (Read) provides much truth about the responsibility of a steward.

    A. The (decision) of what to do with the owner's assets was totally in the hands of the servants. (v.13)

    B. The servants knew the owner expected (a positive return) on what he had invested in them. (v.21)

    C. One's successful (management) of the master's resources determined the reward. (v.17,19,24)

III. According to 1 Corinthians 4:1-2 (Read)

    A. Stewardship involves more than the (management) of money. It also involves how we manage our talents and the truths God has put in our hands.

    B. Stewards are to be (faithful). The word could be translated consistent or steadfast.

God is not interested in having a relationship with us based on convenience. He wants a love based on a commitment to Him during both the good and bad times. How we manage life is important. What we do with our time, talents, finances, and resources indicates the depth of our commitment. A great deal can be discovered about a person by looking at their calendar and checkbook. It will indicate what they really feel to be important.

Financial Stewardship

An important part of our commitment to God has to do with our finance. Where we spend our money is an indication of what is important to us. (Read Matthew 6:19-21)

Discuss: If one is the manager of finances that really belong to another, what are some things you would expect him to do? If Christians are stewards of God's resources, how does what we just talked about apply to them?

There are several obvious things that good financial stewards should do: (Budget, be careful of credit card expenses, pay your bills, etc.)

Introduction to Tithing

One aspect of stewardship is tithing. This is an important Bible concept. The word *tithe* means a tenth. As stewards, we need to know the proper way to tithe, what tithes are, where and to whom it should be paid, what we are to tithe on, and when to tithe. These are some of the questions we will answer from the scriptures. Study your Bible closely on this point so you can be in obedience in your tithing, and so you can give others proof as to the importance of paying tithes.

Tithing is (a tenth of your income or increase). Compare Genesis 14:20 and Hebrews 7:2-4. These verses show Abraham bringing Melchizedek a tithe; a tenth.

IV. The History of Tithing

A. Before the law, Abraham paid tithes to Melchizedek (Genesis 14:20). (Jacob) also promised God the tenth (Genesis 28:22).

B. Under the Law
1. Read Leviticus 27:30-34. (All) the tithe is the Lord's.
2. Read Numbers 18:20-24. Israel's (spiritual leaders) received the tithe.
3. Read Deuteronomy 12:5-6,11,17. Tithes were to be brought to a place (chosen by God).
4. Read Malachi 3:8-10. For one not to tithe was considered (robbery)!

C. Christ teaching on the subject: Read Matthew 23:23. Obviously Jesus was teaching on the hypocrisy of the Scribes and Pharisees. In doing so, He mentions their faithfulness to tithe. Based on His concluding statement referring back to tithing: *". . . and not to leave the other undone."* clearly they were not hypocrites for tithing, but for leaving other things undone. Jesus encouraged them to continue the practice of tithing.

D. Under Grace
1. In Genesis 14:20, (Abraham) paid tithes. According to Galatians 3:7, we who are of (faith) are the (children of Abraham). According to John 8:39, if you are Abraham's children, you will do the work of Abraham.
2. Read Hebrews 7:1-11. Abraham tithed to Melchizedek. The writer points out that here men that die receive tithes (verse 8). This is written in the present tense, indicating that it was occurring even as Hebrews was written in A.D. 64. In the early church people continued to tithe.

Tithing is the Biblical doctrine that teaches us to give 10% of our income or increase (salary, dividends, bonuses, profit from merchandise sales, government benefits, inheritances, court settlements, garden produce, etc.) to support the ministry. It is an essential part of stewardship. A key to being blessed is tithing. When I look at people who are struggling financially, I think, if only you would learn to tithe God could bless you!

Let's operate on the following premises. God is the owner of all our resources, we simply manage them for him. If the owner wishes us to bring 10% of our income to support those who provide us spiritual food and leadership, we should obey.

Carlton L. Coon Sr.   *Bear Fruit – Teacher's Manual*

Session Five - Survey Sheet
"Stewardship"

Name: _____ Date: _____

1. What is a steward?

2. What do you manage for God?

3. What did the poor manager of Luke 19:12-27 do with the things the owner had left in his care? Why was this poor management (stewardship)?

4. What did the good managers do with the owners resources? How does this principle apply to your life?

5. What does our checkbook and calendar tell about us?

6. What is a tithe?

7. What did Christ have to say about tithing?

8. Do you have any questions about this introductory lesson on stewardship?

Session Six
FINANCIAL STEWARDSHIP - TITHING

Goal of This Lesson: To encourage you to make a 12 month commitment to give 10% of your increase. If you make such a commitment, you will be blessed, and it will be the start of a lifelong habit.

Note to Teacher: It has been said: "There are three conversions in the salvation of every man: the conversion of his head, his heart, and his pocketbook. The latter conversion is often the most difficult." When someone is new to the kingdom of God, it is very difficult for them to perceive the importance of managing God's resources in a way to bless his kingdom. This material will take time to cover. Be prepared to answer questions dealing with the subject. You may want to review some of this with your pastor.

I. Review what tithing is, as introduced in last week's lesson.

II. *Note to Teacher:* Preview today's material. This lesson will take a different approach than any we have dealt with. It will attempt to answer many questions you may have about being a good steward and especially about tithing.

III. *Question #1* - What portion of our increase is tithe?

  A. The tithe of Israelites came from the (first fruits) according to Deuteronomy 26.

  B. Tithing should be the (first) thing on the budget. God will bless you accordingly. Some would erroneously believe that they are to pay all their bill and then bring in 10% of what remains. This is not the scriptural pattern.

IV. *Question #2* - What should tithes be used for? The Bible example always had tithes used to financially support those who (blessed or ministered) to the one paying the tithe.

  A. Read Hebrews 7:1-11 and Genesis 14:30. Melchizedek received tithe from Abraham who he had blessed.

  B. Read Numbers 18:20-24. Levites received tithe from the Israelite people who they served.

C. Read 1 Timothy 5:17-18. Paul told Timothy that elders who labor in word and doctrine, are worthy of double honor and are not to be muzzled (uncared for) but "is worthy of his reward" (material things).

Tithes are used to support the pastor, provide salary for evangelists, supplemental pastors, and office staff. Those who oversee the use of tithing must be accountable to God for its use.

V. *Question #3* - Where should I pay my tithes?

   A. According to Deuteronomy 12:5-6, 11 and 17, the tithe was to be paid where (God designated).

   B. Malachi 3:8-10 says to (bring them to the altar) at the house of God.

   C. According to 1 Corinthians 9:1-14, one who sows spiritual things (teaches, preaches, and leads you) reaps carnal (temporal or earthly) things.
      1. He ministers about holy things, therefore, he is to live of the things of the temple and partake of things offered at the altar (verse 13).
      2. Your pastor is like a man planting a vineyard and caring for a flock or a man going to war. A warrior receives help to fight the battle (he cannot bear the expense alone). One who plants eats fruit of the vineyard and a shepherd drinks milk of the flock (verses 7-9).
      3. They which preach the gospel should live of the gospel (verse 14).
      4. You should pay your tithes where you attend church and to the pastor you sit under. The products of a man's efforts and labor go to support him. The pastor sows to you spiritual things and you respond with the temporal. You wouldn't work for a man and him pay someone else would you? Would you plant a crop and not eat any of it but give it to someone else? Would you feed a flock and then not eat the meat and drink the milk? "No!" is the answer to all these questions. How then can you attend a church where you are furnished pews, lights, gas, water, heat, air-conditioning, a pastor, prayer for the sick, counseling in time of need, etc., and then send your tithes and offerings elsewhere? To send your tithes and offerings to a radio or television preacher, an orphanage, another church, to a visiting minister or missionary, a Bible school, or any place other than your local assembly, puts you in a place of disobedience to God.

VI. *Question #4* - How much of my increase is tithes? (10%) *Note to Teacher:* That sounds simple enough, but it is helpful to do several equations where a tenth is calculated. Some calculations of tithe:

A salary check of $350. (The tithe is the first $35.)

Selling a car for $2,000 after buying it for $1,500. In order to determine one's tithe, first calculate the profit. Do this as follows: Sales price less the original purchase price equals profit. So $2,000 less $1,500 equals $500. There was a profit of $500. The tithe on $500 is $50.

Inheriting $40,000. The entire $40,000 is an increase to you. 10% of $40,000 is $4,000. This will be your tithe.

Getting a financial settlement of $1,000,000. After deducting all attorney expenses, tithe 10% of the remainder.

A business where the net profits are $90,000 off gross sales of $600,000. Tithe on the profits for the company. However, if the business provides you benefits that would normally be out of pocket (automobile, fuel, etc.) you really should tithe on those personal increases.

VII. *Question #5* - Should ministers pay tithes? Based on the example of the Levites who paid tithes to the (priests), all full-time and part-time ministers should tithe. Read Numbers 18:26, 32, and Nehemiah 10:37-39.

VIII. *Question #6* - What happens if I don't tithe?

A. Read Malachi 3:8-10.
   1. You put yourself in the position of a (robber).
   2. By doing so, you (close the windows of heaven) on your soul.

B. Read Haggai 1:2-6. Haggai says it is possible to put money in bags with holes in them. This is another tragic loss to the non-tither.

IX. *Question #7* - Can I put my tithes in the offering and it still be considered tithing? As you will hear, there is a distinct difference between the use of tithes and offering. Our offerings are free-will based on our capability, and commitment. These funds are used to support the physical structure and the various outreaches - Bus Ministry, Sunday School, Home Bible Studies, Divorce Recovery, etc. - of the church. *(Note to Teacher:* Select several of the following verses which speak of offerings as being distinct from the tithe: Malachi 3:8-10, Ecclesiastes

5:1-6, 1 Corinthians 16:1-2, 2 Corinthians 8:12-15, 2 Corinthians 9:6-7)

Note to Teacher: Be sure to provide time for questions. Below are some questions you can expect.

1. Should I tithe on my net or my gross? (Discuss the response with your pastor prior to teaching the lesson.)
2. Should I tithe on an inheritance? (We should tithe on all increase.)
3. How should small business owners tithe since their true increase is not usually known until some months after the fact? (Discuss this with your pastor. I have suggested that small business owners tithe an estimated amount until they receive their quarterly statement from their accountant. At that time they can add any funds needed to cover the shortage, or if they have paid more than a tenth, they can make adjustments during the coming quarter.)

Hopefully, this has provided some guidelines to what is an important part of stewardship. (*Note to Teacher:* This is a good opportunity to pass out the envelopes used by the church to collect tithes and offerings. Quite often newcomers will not know that they should distinguish what they are giving.) In the past, when I've taught this material, I've ended with a challenge: Let me encourage you to be faithful in tithing and see if God does not respond in a positive manner. As a matter of fact, I challenge you to tithe for twelve months. If you have not been blessed, I will personally return your money with ten percent interest. God is faithful to keep his promises.

Carlton L. Coon Sr.   Bear Fruit – Teacher's Manual

Session Six - Survey Sheet
"Financial Stewardship - Tithing"

Name: _____ Date: _____

1. What portion of your increase is tithe? Does God get the leavings or should we bring him the first portion? Provide a scriptural reference.

2. What should the tithe be used for? Provide a scriptural reference.

3. What is the message of 1 Corinthians 9:1-14?

4. Calculate the tithe on the following:

    a. A bi-weekly payroll check of $400.
    b. The sell of a house. It was purchased for $40,000, $10,000 was spent on repairs, and it sold for $70,000.
    c. You receive an inheritance of $10,000.

5. According to Haggai 1:2-6 and Malachi 3:8-10 what happens when one does not tithe?

6. Read Malachi 3:8-10, Ecclesiastes 5:1-6, 1 Corinthians 16:1-2, 2 Corinthians 8:12-15. Now write a simple explanation of the difference between tithe and offering.

7. Is there any part of this lesson you would like to have reviewed?

Carlton L. Coon Sr.   *Bear Fruit – Teacher's Manual*

Session Seven
FINANCIAL STEWARDSHIP - GIVING

Goal of This Lesson: Distinguish between tithe and offerings. Giving the students a stable basis on which to plan their giving.

I. As we have discovered, Biblical stewardship means we are not owners of any of our possessions, but rather manage them on behalf of God, the true owner. In the last lesson, the concept of tithing was covered thoroughly. Discuss: What do you remember from our discussion about tithing? Tithing is a tenth of our income or increase that is given to God's work for the purpose of supporting the five-fold ministry (pastors, apostles, prophets, teachers, and evangelists). It is to provide support to those who sow spiritual things in our life.

II. Offerings are a different concept, with a different purpose and objective.

III. Offerings are (free-will). Notice how these worked in Bible history.

    A. Read Exodus 35:4-5. Israel brought offerings to build the tabernacle. Notice that it was not built from their tithing. In their giving, the task was bigger than one person alone could accomplish.

        1. Read Exodus 35:20-29. It details the need.
        2. Read Exodus 36:5-7. This is the result of their giving

    B. Offerings are used for the building, use, and maintenance of God's work. If (everyone) does their part, it is easy on everyone.

IV. Our (attitude) is as important as our (action).

    A. Read Matthew 6:1-4.
        1. Do not give (to be seen of men).
        2. Offerings should be (private).

    B. Read 1 Corinthians 16:2. (Consistency) in giving is essential. Our offerings are consistently needed to support the ongoing needs of the church. From a common sense perspective, it is obvious that sporadic offerings puts the church in a difficult budgetary position. Offerings should be part of your planned budget.

    C. Read 2 Corinthians 8:11. Don't just (talk about) and desire to give, saying, "When I make more money, gain inheritance . . .". Instead, give out of what you have now. My observation is that those who do not give when they have little also do not give when they have an abundance.

    D. Read 2 Corinthians 9:6-7.
1. The appropriate approach is to (purpose in your heart) what you will give.
2. Giving should always be done (cheerfully). The Greek word "cheerful" is *hilarion* which could be translated hilarious. In essence, God loves *giggling* givers. In 1 Chronicles 29:9 the people rejoiced because they had given willingly.
3. Giving is not to be the result of (necessity).

    E. Read Mark 12:41-44. It's not (how much you give) but how much you have left that God looks at.

V. Giving is a grace. Read 2 Corinthians 8:1-8.

    A. Money is not the ultimate end. Paul sought men rather than money. (verses 1-3)

    B. Paul did not propose any indirect methods of raising money. The Corinthian believers were very poor. Beyond doubt, bazaars, festivals, and rummage sales would have brought excellent returns. Paul made no mention of these easy sources of money. He was specific, "Upon the first day of the week let every one of you lay by him in store, as God hath prospered him, that there be no gatherings when I come." (1 Corinthians 16:2)

VI. There are some things that Paul did to encourage people to give:

    A. He declared the (grace of the Lord Jesus). (2 Corinthians 8:9) What greater incentive could there be to give? From riches to poverty, Jesus had gone for them that they might go from poverty to riches.

    B. He told of abounding (liberality of other saints). Of the saints in Macedonia, Paul seems to be saying, "They were so poor that I really didn't want them to give, but they begged me for an opportunity to give."

    C. He motivated them to give by (presenting the need) of the saints in Jerusalem. A sure incentive for giving is the good our giving will do. There is a missionary need, there is a need to be able to evangelize our local community.

    D. Paul assured them that all gifts would be honestly used and handled.

VII. The motivation to give.

   A. Paul appealed to the self-respect of the Corinthians. He points out the shame they would feel if others came by and found them unprepared to give. "Men will not respect us, and we cannot respect ourselves, if we do not give." - (J. Broadus)

> You can give without loving,
> but you cannot love without giving.

   B. Paul urged them to finish a worthy task which was worthily begun. (2 Corinthians 8:10-11) We should complete churches; we should pay bills; we should advance the cause of missions. The work is not finished; it is only just begun.

   C. A further motive is the reward which is sure to come. (2 Corinthians 8:14, 9:10) There will come a day when you will need a blessing.
      1. Pledges were taken beforehand. Paul talks of their afore-promised bounty.
      2. Care and help were provided toward redeeming the pledges made. He followed up.
      3. Offerings were to be made with system and regularity.
      4. Carefully chosen messengers were to take the offering to Jerusalem. (1 Corinthians 16:3)

VIII. Why should we give to God's work?

   A. We should give because of God's grace to us.

   B. We should give because of the blessing the church has been to us. Discuss: How has the church blessed your family?

   C. We should give because we are so instructed in God's word.

   D. We should give because giving will result in our being blessed.
      1. Read Luke 6:38. Give and it shall be (given) . . .
      2. Read Malachi 3:8-10.
      3. Your financial blessing will greatly depend on your decision to give.

   E. We should give because it takes money to move the gospel.

IX. How much should I give?

   A. The church cannot function unless the people plan to give. Planned giving is not dropping one dollar in the offering pan each time it goes by. Planned giving is determining in your mind, "I will give 'X' amount of my finances to missions, building fund, general fund, Sunday School, etc." or "I will give this percentage of my income to offerings."

   B. Some churches suggest that offerings equal five percent of an individual's income. The Bible indicates this to be what Israel did. Regardless of whether you decide to give a certain <u>amount</u> or a specific <u>percentage</u> of your income, it is important that you commit to something.

X. Offering Options

   A. Our church is an evangelistic congregation that puts much money into meeting needs and evangelizing our world.

      1. <u>World Missions</u> offerings are used to support missionaries in America and around the world.
      2. <u>Sunday School</u> - These funds are spent to provide literature for ministering to children, improving the classrooms, and supplementing the evangelistic outreach of Bus Ministry.
      3. <u>Building Fund</u> - These funds are currently being set aside in preparation of expanding our auditorium and educational space.
      4. <u>Bus Ministry</u> - These funds are given specifically to support the bringing of adults and children to Sunday School. This is a positive evangelistic outreach.
      5. <u>General Fund</u> - These monies pay the utility bills, insurance, and normal maintenance fees. It is from this fund that we pay the monthly notes secured by the church property.

There are other ministries and needs. Youth, Campus Ministry, Radio Ministry, etc. can always use your support.

Regardless of your giving, we pledge to use appropriate accountability and be good stewards. The church books are open to the fullest extent possible and yet maintain individual privacy. Each year we provide a financial statement detailing funds received and spent. If you have questions, see the pastor or church secretary.

Carlton L. Coon Sr.   *Bear Fruit – Teacher's Manual*

Session Seven - Survey Sheet
"Financial Stewardship - Giving"

Name: _____ Date: _____

1. In Exodus 35 and 36, Israel is invited to give to meet a need. What was that need? How did the people respond?

2. What should our attitude be toward giving? Provide a scriptural reference.

3. What is the lesson of 1 Corinthians 16:2 about giving?

4. What should the emotional state of the giver be, according to 2 Corinthians 9?

5. What did Paul do to encourage people to give?

6. When you consider the various offerings that the church receives, which one(s) inspire you to give?

7. Write out Luke 6:38 in your own words.

8. Is there any part of this lesson you would like to have covered more thoroughly?

Session Eight
THE LIFESTYLE OF A CHRISTIAN, PART I

Goal of This Lesson: Introduce the student to some truths about holy and righteous living. This material is intended to keep us from attitudes of self-righteousness. This lesson will be followed by more specific truths.

Note to Teacher: Of all the material covered, this will need the most input from your pastor. As a matter of fact, he may have lesson material he would like to substitute for the next two lessons. The disciplines, guidelines, and standards are so unique to a congregation and pastor that it is imperative that you have your pastor review this.

Introduction

This day is one of tremendous challenge to the church. Satan is going about as a roaring lion seeking whom he may devour. Yet the devil is intelligent enough to know that we cannot be trapped in a single day. It is his plan to compromise principles of righteousness that seemingly would have little meaning and, thus, gradually lead us down the road to doom. This must not be allowed to happen. It is in this spirit that I bring to you the truths of these lessons on the lifestyle of a Christian. The lessons will have several objectives:

Objective 1 - Clearly define holiness

Objective 2 - Determine what sets the Christian apart

Objective 3 - Determine our responsibility in being holy, including the pastor's role

Objective 4 - Explain the following disciplines of the Church:
    A. Sexual distinction
    B. Apparel
    C. Jewelry
    D. Makeup
    E. What one allows in his or her mind.

Objective 5 - Deal with principles of doctrine, cultural factors, church standards, and personal convictions

I.   Discuss: Perhaps you have heard the word *holy* applied to someone or something. What does that word mean? (The word means for one to be, "set apart unto God.") Several different terms used in the Bible come from the same basic root. The Hebrew word, which with its various derivatives, was translated as holy, sanctified, and sanctification is a word which <u>Strong's Concordance</u> defines as *a consecrated thing, a dedicated thing, or something or someone hallowed.* The Greek word and its derivatives, which gives us the same term, is a word meaning: (most) holy (one, thing), saint.

II. The importance of sanctification

   A. From the perspective of God, (note that this is not from the perspective of man) three things are absolutely necessary for one to be saved. These three things are justification, regeneration, and sanctification. In Pentecost we talk much and preach much about regeneration. The new birth is an important essential, but regeneration does not exclude the need to be declared just (justified) before God. Nor does it exclude the necessity of being sanctified - set apart unto God.

   B. Sanctification is a Biblical and theological term. It is the condition of right relationship with God. For the sake of this lesson, let's say that the term <u>holy</u> is the practical application of abstract theology. It is life actions and life relationships. To be holy is to be sanctified.

   C. We must understand the balance between holiness and justification. The Pharisees were living outwardly sanctified lives, yet inwardly were full of dead men's bones. It is possible to place such an emphasis on one's distinction from the world as to reach a point where we believe that our own goodness can save us or please God! It is not so. Every man will be justified by faith. However, sanctification that is not self-righteousness pleases God and is a necessary part of our walk with God.

III. What sets apart or *sanctifies* a Christian?

   A. Read Colossians 1:21-22. We are sanctified through Christ's death.

   B. Read Romans 15:16. We Gentiles are sanctified by the Holy Ghost.

   C. Read 1 Corinthians 6:11. Sanctification comes through the name and by the spirit.

   D. Read John 17:19 and Ephesians 5:25. The truth sanctifies.

   E. The things that set us apart in God's sight are: Christ's death, the Holy Ghost, the name of Jesus, and the truth of God's word.

IV. There are those who would have you believe that the work of sanctification is complete. However, the Greek tenses indicate that the work of sanctification is ongoing. Whenever someone is born again, they are immediately set apart unto God by the things previously mentioned. Even thought their lifestyle may not be in keeping with Christ's plan, they are holy. As time passes, and the new convert is taught the principles of Christian living, their lifestyle should change to reflect the inner work of sanctification that has taken place and is continuing. When one teaches about the lifestyle advocated by Paul and the early apostles; things that reach across time and culture to distinguish the Christian; the question is often asked, "Is this a heaven or hell issue?" I'll be honest enough to say, "I don't know." However, I can affirm that they are indications of one's Christian maturity. I believe one can illustrate it like this: If a couple have a baby who they eventually discover is mentally handicapped, they continue to love that baby and retain it in the family. However, that child does not mature like a normal child. The fact of that baby's limitation means it cannot do some of the things more mature children do. It has limitations. A lack of a Christian lifestyle, likewise limits a person's right to a leadership role, or to responsibilities that require them to be on the platform.

Taylor said, "When the fixed standard of God's holiness is properly regarded, moral evaluations can be made which are in harmony with the good. However, if the standard becomes flexible instead of fixed, the product is moral relativism. Good and evil are mixed together in a nebulous mist that allows each person to decide for himself what is right or wrong." Simply put:

We must get back to some absolutes!

Sanctification or holiness is God separating one from his natural love of sin and the world; putting a new principle in his heart, and making him Godly in conduct. The instrument God uses to accomplish this is his Word. Another important factor in our being separate from the world is the watchful eye and warning voice of the local Shepherd.

V. The Christian who has only just been born-again is sanctified. Being set apart to God is a work that mankind cannot accomplish within himself. Yet the ongoing work of sanctification takes the application of my life doing God's will.

    A. Read Hebrews 4:11. We are called to (labor).

    B. Read Hebrews 12:1. Christians are commanded to lay aside (weights and sins).

VI. Three important reasons we should be holy:

   A. Read 1 Peter 1:13. We are to be holy because (God is holy).
      1. "Gird up the loins of your mind" indicates a protected and prepared state of mind.
      2. Note that Christians are not to fashion themselves after their former life-style.
      3. How is God holy? In everything: creation, redemption, justification, etc. Everything God does is holy! We are to be holy as He is holy. We should be holy in everything we do.
      4. The word *conversation* effectively means life-style. We are to be holy in our life-style.

   B. Read 2 Peter 3:9-10. We should desire to be holy because Jesus Christ is coming back for a (holy church).

   C. Read Hebrews 12:14. Without holiness, no man shall (see the Lord).

VII. So what is my responsibility in living a holy life?

   A. Read 2 Corinthians 7:1. We are to cleanse ourselves from all filthiness of the flesh and spirit.
      1. Discuss: What is filthiness of the flesh? filthiness of the Spirit?
      2. Notice who it is that does the cleansing. We are to cleanse ourselves!
      3. Said Oscar Wilde, "The devil was once crossing the Libyan desert, and he came upon a spot where a number of small fiends were tormenting a holy hermit. The sainted man easily shook off their evil suggestions. The devil watched their failure, and then he stepped forward to give them a lesson. 'What you do is too crude'; he said. 'Permit me for one moment.' With that he whispered to the holy man, 'Your brother has just been made Bishop of Alexandria.' A scowl of malignant jealousy at once clouded the serene face of the hermit. 'That,' said the devil to his imps, 'is the sort of thing which I should recommend.'" (This is an illustration of filthiness of the spirit.)

   B. Read Romans 12:1-2. We are to present our bodies as (living sacrifices). Notice the presenting of one's body as a living sacrifice is dependent on the renewing of his mind. Holiness cannot focus on the outer man, the bigger battle is for the mind!

C. Read 1 Corinthians 3:16. Our bodies are to be kept as holy temples. Discuss: What are things that might defile the temple of God? What are things that just don't seem to go with being Christ-like? These defile the temple of the Holy Ghost.

In this introductory material, we have seen the balance between regeneration, sanctification, and justification. We have observed that sanctification is twofold. I am sanctified by the death of Christ, the Holy Ghost, the name of Jesus, and the truth. I am being sanctified (made holy) as I progressively grow in my relationship with God.

Carlton L. Coon Sr. Bear Fruit – Teacher's Manual

Session Eight - Survey Sheet
"The Lifestyle of a Christian, Part I"

Name: _____ Date: _____

1. What does the word *holy* mean?

2. From God's perspective, what are the three things that must happen for us to be saved? Define justified. Define sanctified. Define regenerated.

3. In God's sight, what five things set us apart from the world? Give scripture references.

4. What is your responsibility now that you are saved?

5. What does 1 Peter 1 teach about holiness?

6. Write 2 Peter 3:9-10 in your own words.

7. How do we cleanse ourselves of filthiness of the flesh and spirit?

8. Is there any part of this lesson you would like to have covered in more detail?

Session Nine
THE LIFESTYLE OF A CHRISTIAN, PART II

Goal of This Lesson: To provide a stronger foundation for our concept of holiness. Further to help us to comprehend the pastor's role in our life.

Note to Teacher: Please be reminded, this material requires the review of your pastor before you teach it. In this lesson we get into some specific issues. Your pastor may have additional thoughts he would like you to share as you teach this lesson.

I. The maturing of a child involves discipline. This discipline involves instruction, correction, and guidance. Hopefully, the discipline by a parent leads to the child's self-discipline. Much of what we will discuss in this lesson deals with the discipline of Christian living. This is instructing us in a life that will please God.

Note to Teacher: You may want to point out to your students that the material we cover in this lesson is not progressive. Instead, separate cords of truth are laid out and then intertwined into a rope.

II. What kind of church do you suppose God wants?

    A. Read 2 Corinthians 11:2. A (chaste virgin).

    B. Read Ephesians 5:26-27. A (glorious) church without (spot) or (blemish).

    C. *Note to Teacher:* The first strand of truth: God wants his people to be clean and pure.

III. How does one know who's Lord of his life?

    A. Read Luke 6:46. And why call ye me (Lord) and (do not) the things that I say.

    B. *Note to Teacher:* A second strand of truth: Our relationship with God is not based on what we say, but rather our obedience to the instructions of the Lord. As Pastor Phillip White of Burbank, California once preached, "If He Can't Say No, then He's Not Lord!"

IV. The Principle of Authority and Submission:

A. Read Leviticus 10:10. The priest had the responsibility of determining between the holy and the unholy. The priest determined what was acceptable and what was not acceptable.

B. Read Hebrews 13:17. As New Testament church members, we are called on to obey them that rule over us for they watch for our souls. Who is it that rules over you? Who is it that watches for your soul?

C. *Note to Teacher:* This is the third strand of truth: God has placed authoritative leadership in his church to set some guidelines to protect his people. Remember, your pastor serves as a watchman to warn you of impending danger. Because of the position God has put him in, he may see things as being dangerous that you do not.

Applying the Principle

In Matthew 16:19 and 18:18, Jesus showed the authority He would put in His Church. In Matthew 16:19, He responded to Peter's declaration, "Thou art the Christ, the Son of the living God." The Church would be built on the foundation of Jesus' deity, and Peter would be given the keys, or would be the spokesman. In Matthew 18:18, Jesus is speaking about handling disputes and disagreements that would arise in the Church.

In all likelihood, Jesus is saying: "Simon Peter, the Church will grow beyond the boundaries of its current cultural setting, and will spread across the earth. It will reach to every nation and generation. With this growth, there will be some necessary adjustments. I leave you the principles of My Word, but people will want to know how these principles are to be practically applied to them. There is not a 'Thou shalt' or 'Thou shalt not,' for every situation that will arise. This will require some decisions by your leaders. You will have to pray, read your Bible, view the cultural setting, take counsel together, trust the guiding of the Holy Ghost, and then make decisions on what these principles mean to your people. You will have to determine that some things are permissible and others not. Whatever you bind (declare wrong) in earth, will be considered wrong in heaven. Whatever you loose (declare allowable and permissible), will be considered allowable in heaven. I will stand behind your decisions, because I am going to lead My people through you."

Let me show the necessity of this: Our United States of America has a constitution, but we do not have the right to decide how that constitution should be applied to us. The result would be nothing but chaos. Therefore, we have branches of government that makes decisions on how the principles of the constitution should be applied to the lives of the citizens. These are the legislative and judicial branches. It is no different in the church. Christian leaders have to make some practical decisions concerning our faith in our culture.

The issues faced, and decisions made will vary from culture to culture, and from generation to generation. A big issue faced by heathen converts in some cities was whether they should buy the meat that had been sacrificed on the altars in idol temples. This meat could be bought on the "black market" much cheaper. This was an important point for poor believers to consider. Idols were nothing, so the meat was not in any way contaminated. But the Christians would be supporting a corrupt system by buying at the meat market. Such actions also might cause another Christian to stumble in his relationship with God if he saw them buying food from the temple from which he had just been saved. So the leaders had to decide how the principles of God's Word would apply in this setting. The decision that was made is not even an issue today. It was a tradition that was established in that time for that issue.

Another important decision the leaders had to make concerned these same Gentile converts. In Acts 15, the expanding Church faced a crisis that could have permanently divided it. Some of the Jews demanded that the Gentiles were not saved unless they were circumcised. Paul disagreed, asserting that Christ had fulfilled the law, and the believers were free in Christ. What decision could the leaders make? Probably none that would please everyone. But that is one of the prices of leadership. It is necessary to make some tough decisions! For the leadership to do nothing would surely have divided the Church.

In council, they earnestly discussed this situation. "In the multitude of counselors, there is safety." (Proverbs 11:14; 15:22; 24:6) In dealing with this issue, they had no specific instructions from Jesus. Should they follow the laws for those who converted from idols to Judaism, or did Christ fulfill the law? The leaders heard both sides of the issue, prayed, and took final advice from James. James, who was the leader, finally stated the direction the church would go. He settled the issue. They determined some guidelines but did not impose circumcision on the Gentiles. Letters were written and sent to the local churches (Acts 16:4) describing what they considered to be right and what was forbidden. In Acts 15:28 they wrote, "For it seemed good to the Holy Ghost and to us to lay upon you no greater burden than these necessary things." In John 16:14 Jesus had promised that the Holy Ghost would lead and guide them into all truth and show them things to come. The Spirit helped them make the right decision. What these leaders bound in earth was bound in heaven, and what they loosed in earth as permissible, was loosed in heaven.

Likewise, Godly leaders face decisions their early counterparts never faced, and will have to follow the same procedure.

Note to Teacher: This is another strand of truth. The leader in a congregation is to make decisions that are based on the principles of scripture and the wisdom of council. These cultural decisions are to be abided by.

V. What is the difference between personal convictions, church standards, and Biblical principles?

- A. Bible truths are things for which there can be no compromise among the saints. These are things which time does not change. The moral instructions of the law would fit this category.

- B. (Bible principles) are things for which the Bible doesn't get specific. However, it gives a direction for us to follow morally and ethically.

- C. (Church standards) are determined by the pastor. Leadership appointed by God for a particular congregation. These are based on Bible principles. A pastor is accountable to God for them.

- D. A (personal conviction) is a conviction an individual has laid upon them personally by God. It would be akin to the Nazarite vow of the Old Testament - something they are responsible for but should hold no one else accountable for (Numbers 6). If they do hold others responsible, their attitude is Pharisaical.

VI. Bible Truth - General Principles of Holiness

- A. Read Romans 12:1-2. Be not (conformed) to this world.

- B. Read Romans 13:14. Make no (provision for the flesh) to fulfill the lusts thereof.

- C. Read 2 Corinthians 6:17. Come out and be (separate).

- D. Read 1 Thessalonians 5:22. (Forsake the appearance of evil.)

Note to Teacher: Conclude the class with prayer, asking God to begin to put into the heart of the students a desire for their life to be set apart unto God.

Carlton L. Coon Sr. Bear Fruit – Teacher's Manual

Session Nine - Survey Sheet
"The Lifestyle of a Christian, Part II"

Name: _____ Date: _____

1. What does scripture liken Christ's church to?

2. What does the saying, "Jesus is Lord over my life." mean? What does it mean if we are disobeying the things his word teaches?

3. (This answer was not covered in the lesson. You will have to do some research.) In what relationships is submission called for?

4. Write Hebrews 13:17 in your own words.

5. What does it mean to, ". . . obey them that have the rule over you. . .?"

6. Why is a Christian not to be conformed to this world?

7. What does the Bible mean when it says, "Make no provision for the flesh to fulfill the lusts thereof?"

8. Are there any things in this lesson you would like to have reviewed?

Session Ten
SPECIFIC PRINCIPLES OF CHRISTIAN LIVING

Goal of This Lesson: To provide some specific scriptural based guidelines on how Christians should live their life.

Note to Teacher: Again, be sure to have the pastor review this lesson. It is possible that he may wish to replace all or part of this material. You may need to take two sessions to cover this material.

I. Review the general principles from the past two lessons.

II. It is a very rare thing to hear of a church that attempts to teach people about the distinctive lifestyle that the Bible calls for Christians to live. During this session, you will probably hear things that are brand new to you. It is important to have your mind open to receive God's direction for your life. Remember:

   A. He is your Lord only if you obey Him and His word.

   B. Christians are called to be a separated people.

III. Seven Important Principles

   A. <u>Principle #1</u> - The clothes you wear is an expression of what you are. Read Proverbs 7:10, and 1 Timothy 2:8-10. This principle can be illustrated by the many different uniforms people wear for different types of employment. What they wear says something about them. When people go out for a night on the town, they really dress up, often putting on their most immodest and "sexiest" clothes. You see, external appearance has a profound impact on the inner self. It molds our feelings and expectations.

   > The Tyndale New Testament Commentaries says in commenting on 1 Timothy 2:8-10, "Paul was shrewd enough to know that a woman's dress is a mirror of her mind. Outward ostentation is not in keeping with a prayerful and devout attitude."

   B. <u>Principle #2</u> - The Christian should not seek attention by things like jewelry, and expensive clothing, but rather, is to be distinguished by a meek and quiet spirit. (Read 1 Peter 3:1-5) Ultimately, ungodly dress impacts society as a whole by teaching false values to everyone.

   C. <u>Principle #3</u> - The way we dress has spiritual significance for us and

others.
1. We are known by our fruit. Read Matthew 7:16-20.
2. We must appear right before others. Read Romans 12:17 and 2 Corinthians 8:21.
3. Adultery begins in the eye and heart. Psychologists tell us the male sex drive is often triggered by visual stimuli alone. In our age of sexual promiscuity and liberation, this has probably become increasingly true of females. Many people do not realize the degree to which the way they dress affects those they come in contact with. (Read Matthew 5:28 to discover the implications of lustful thought.)

D. <u>Principle #4</u> - Extravagant clothes, jewelry, and such are very poor investments. As stewards, we are to manage the finance for God. (Luke 16:10-13, 12:33-34)

E. <u>Principle #5</u> - Immodest clothing, jewelry, and makeup feed the lust of the flesh (1 John 2:16). When tempted to dress in an immodest way, one should question his or her motives by asking, "Whose attention am I trying to get?"

F. <u>Principle #6</u> - Immodest clothing, jewelry, and makeup appeal to the lust of the eyes. It was the lust of the eyes that captivated Eve when she looked at the tree of knowledge of good and evil.

G. <u>Principle #7</u> - Immodest clothing, jewelry, and makeup cater to the pride of life.

Note to Teacher: The remainder of this lesson gives you an abundance of verses dealing with each subject. There is no way to read all of these in a lesson. However, it is essential to read a representative sampling and encourage your students to read the remainder of them at home.

If the Bible repeatedly speaks negatively about a particular subject, it is safe to say that it is not viewed in a positive way by God. We are going to view a sampling of verses dealing with each of these subjects. This sampling gives us a Biblical principle. In each case the Bible adds no verses of a positive nature to counter the negatives.

IV. Biblical Examples - Immodesty

A. Genesis 3:7, 21<u>(Adam and Eve)</u> discovered they were naked. God gave them a covering.

B. Leviticus 18:6-19 Uncovering nakedness is an Old Testament expression for a sexual relationship.

    C. Genesis 38:14-19 Particular types of clothing are associated with immoral conduct. (Proverbs 7:10)

V. Biblical Examples - Makeup

    A. Without exception, the Bible always associates the use of makeup with wicked women. Further, a study of history indicates that the original use of makeup was by prostitutes to seduce their customers.

    B. 2 Kings 9:30 is Jezebel attempting to seduce Jehu.

    C. Proverbs 6:25 is Solomon's warning to young men about the painted woman.

    D. Jeremiah 4:30 speaks of the waste of Israel preparing herself like a woman making up, when God is not pleased with them.

    E. In Ezekiel 23:40 making up was part of the seduction of men of other nations.

VI. Biblical Examples - Jewelry

    A. Jewelry is often associated with a proud attitude, an immoral lifestyle, or pagan worship.

    B. Genesis 35:1-7 shows that Jacob got rid of idols and earrings before he returned to Bethel.

    C. In Exodus 33:4-6, 35:22 Israel was commanded to take off their ornaments.

    D. Judges 8:24-27 shows that the Ishmaelites and Midianites were distinguished from Israel by their use of jewelry.

    E. In Jeremiah 4:30, God likens backslidden Israel to a jewelry bedecked women.

    F. Hosea 2:13 says Israel was like a woman seducing her lovers with jewelry.

    G. In Esther 2:12-15, Esther was allowed to bedeck herself with anything. She chose to go with oil and perfumes rather than the elaborate jewelry and makeup that was available.

VII. Application - Modesty

    A. What is immodest? According to 1 Timothy 2:9, (Read) some clothing is immodest. Much in the way of clothing for both men and women is only a step away from nudity - miniskirts, shorts, halters, tank tops, beach wear. These must be considered immodest.

    B. In Isaiah 47:2-3, (Read) God considered baring the leg and uncovering the thigh to be a shameful exposure of nakedness. This gives us a basic idea of what God regards as the minimum standard of modesty.

    C. The guidelines which have been established for our people are that:
        1. Clothing for men and women is to be <u>(over the knee)</u>.
        2. Sleeves should be <u>(near the elbow)</u>.
        3. <u>(Low necklines)</u> should be avoided.
        4. Clothes that are <u>(tight)</u> should be avoided by both men and women.
        5. Clothing should have substance. <u>(See through garments)</u> are more seductive than modest.
        6. Both men and women should carry themselves (walk, talk, mannerisms, etc.) as modest Christians.

VIII. Application - Adornment

    A. We should avoid outward adornment that attracts attention to the ornament or decoration. True Godly adornment is in having a meek or quiet spirit.

    B. We do not wear luxurious and expensive clothing. Christians should look as good as possible but should not allow their clothing to gather more attention than their Christ-like spirit.

    C. There are several questions to consider when it comes to clothing.
        1. What is my motive for wearing it? Do I wear it out of pride, a desire to be noticed, or a desire to provoke envy?
        2. Is this wise stewardship on my part? How does it compare with the time and money I spend for necessities, for my family, for the church?
        3. How do others view it? Do they see it as flaunting wealth, making a show, as a manifestation of pride, or an object of envy? Do they see it as inconsistent with the Bible's stand on ornamentation?
        4. What would Jesus do? Would He wear it? Would He spend

His time and money in this fashion?

D. If we answer these questions with honesty and true self-examination, we will never have a problem wearing clothes that are immodest or overly expensive.

IX. Being Set Apart in what You See and Hear

A. The two most oft used gates to the mind are the eyes and ears. If you have the physical ability to see and hear, you are affected by what you see and hear.

B. This being true, as saints we are to guard what we both see and hear. Several scripture references are cited later, but let me issue the warning that you cannot read books and magazines that are unbecoming to Christians and retain your spirituality.

C. Neither can you voluntarily behold (some things we see we do not desire to see and do not make it a point to see them) ungodly things, and retain a spiritual walk with God. This is why we have long preached against the evils of most Hollywood productions. For a saint (in the home where both the husband and wife are saved) to spend many hours watching a television set is to completely ignore the Bible, your better judgment, the judgment of educators, doctors, psychologists and statesmen. The reason: Everything the Bible teaches against is portrayed on T.V. Note the liquor advertisements, divorce, murder, deceit, illicit love affairs, crime, nudity, evil speaking, (swearing and cursing), and etc. that is displayed, and ask yourself how can you spend hours watching this instrument that brings all of this to you.

D. To open our ears (voluntarily) to filthy talk, gossip, ungodly music (all music that is not gospel is not necessarily evil) will not help you spiritually. Remember our bodies are temples of the Holy Ghost, and all the above mentioned things affect that temple. Are you keeping the temple of God undefiled? Note these scriptures on what we see and read:
   1. Matthew 6:22 - The light of the body is the eye.
   2. Psalms 101:3 - I will set no wicked thing before mine eyes.
   3. Psalms 25:15 - My eyes are forever toward the Lord.
   4. Ecclesiastes 1:8 - The eye is not satisfied with seeing.
   5. Joshua 7:20-21 - What Achan saw affected him.
   6. 2 Samuel 11:2-4 - What David saw produced adultery.
   7. Genesis 3:6 - The forbidden fruit was "pleasant to the eyes."
   8. 1 John 3:15-17 - The "lust of the eye" is a part of the world.

9. 2 Peter 2:14 - We can have "... eyes full of adultery."
10. Matthew 5:28 - Looking on a woman and lusting after her constitutes adultery in the heart.
11. 1 Timothy 4:13 - We are to give attendance to reading the Word of God.
12. 1 Timothy 2:15 - Study to shew ourselves approved to God.
13. Revelation 1:3 - "Blessed is he that readeth . . ." (Colossians 4:16, 1 Thessalonians 5:27).
14. John 5:39 - Search the scriptures.
15. Acts 19:19 - Men of Ephesus burned their books that were evil. This would be a good idea for many in our day.

X. What we hear affects us as well.

A. Below are verses dealing with what we allow to enter through the door of our ears.
 1. Romans 10:17 - Faith comes by hearing (Word of God).
 2. Mark 4:24 - Take heed what ye hear.
 3. Luke 8:8 - Take heed how ye hear.
 4. Revelation 2:7 - He that hath an ear let him hear what the spirit sayeth.
 5. 1 Timothy 1:4 - Neither give heed to fables (Titus 1:14).

B. By listening to Satan, the world was plunged into sin. What you hear affects you in many ways. Let's be quick to hear good things and close our ears to the evil.

XI. Being set apart in where you go and what you do

A. Where you take your physical body, and your actions, tell a great story to the world. This is why we must remain separate from the world. We are in this world, but we are not to be a part of it. We are to love sinners, but not sin. We are to be an example to others, but not go the places the world goes and do the things they do. This does not in itself project a holier-than-thou or a better-than-you spirit, but simply stated, we are separating ourselves from sin. We must ever maintain a separated position in this life.
 1. John 17:15 - Jesus said we would not be taken out of the world, but kept from evil.
 2. 2 Corinthians 6:14-18, 7:1 - Study this call for separation very closely.
 3. Hosea 7:8 - The curse of Ephraim was that he mixed among foreign people. Israel was never to mingle with the world; they were a separate people.
 4. 1 Peter 2:11 - We are pilgrims and strangers in this world.

We are not at home here.
5. 1 Peter 4:1-4 - Study this portion of scripture.
6. Judges 15 & 16 - Samson's troubles were caused by mixing himself with the Philistines (worldly people).
7. 1 John 2:15-17 - We are not to love the world.
8. 1 Kings 11:1-8 - Solomon's heart was turned from God by many strange wives.

XII. Clear Sexual Distinction

A. God's word consistently maintains a clear distinction between men and women. The reason for there to be such a clear definition can easily be seen by examining our "uni-sex" culture where homosexuality is quickly becoming accepted as an alternate life-style. The distinctions that are specified in the Bible are expressed in two ways.

B. These two are (hair) and (clothing).

C. Bible Truth about sexual distinction as expressed by hair. (Read 1 Corinthians 11:1-16.) Several terms need defining:
1. Verses 4-6 use the term *covered* repeatedly without defining what the *covering* is. Verse 15 says that (hair) is given for a covering. Therefore, verses 4-6 are referring to hair when the word covering is used.
2. Shorn means (cut, trimmed, or made shorter).

D. Men were taught to cut their hair as a mark of distinction (verses 4, 14).
1. Long hair dishonoreth the man's head. It dishonors the individual, but it also dishonors Christ, who is the spiritual head of the man.
2. Nature teaches it is a shame for a man to have long hair. We accept shorn, shaven, or bald men; it's natural.
3. How long is too long: Men should keep on getting their hair cut. The guideline does not require us to be extreme but to clearly be a man.

E. Women were taught to leave their hair uncut as a mark of distinction. There are six reasons why a woman should leave her hair long and uncut.
1. So she is always *covered*. What does it mean for a woman to be "not covered?" It means she is (shorn). Paul likened being shorn to being shaven. In other words, "the woman's hair had been cut."
2. Because praying or prophesying with an uncovered head

(Remember the covering refers to hair) (dishonoreth her head); physically her own body, spiritually her husband. Paul said she so dishonoreth her head that she had just as well be shaven. Isaiah 3:17, 24 gives a negative perspective of female baldness, as does most of society today.

    3. To be shorn or shaven is a (shame). (Verse 6)

    4. In verse 10, the scripture says the woman should have "power" on her head. Verse five speaks of prayer. Submission to this provides a woman power in prayer.

    5. Because it signifies to the Angels that she remains in submission to her (husband). (Verses 7-12) So the Angels should stay in submission to the Lord.

    6. Because long hair is a (glory) to the woman. (Verse 15)

F. How long is long? The Greek term for long basically means continuing to grow - never getting shorter. This would signify long as being uncut!

XIII. Bible Truth about sexual distinction as expressed by clothing.

A. Read 1 Timothy 2:9. Women are to be adorned in (modest apparel). The Greek word for modest apparel is *katastole*. It means a long robe. At this time, a man wore a *stole* or robe. It reached to slightly below the knee. Women were to wear a *katastole* or long robe. Even though both wore robes, there was quite a distinction between the two.

B. Read Deuteronomy 22:5.

    1. An abomination in God's sight is moral in nature. Only six things in the writings of Moses were spoken of as abominations in God's sight. Each of the six is something that a Christian would still consider a thing hated. The only one some of Christian society has put under attack is Deuteronomy 22:5. The six abominations are:
       a. Homosexuality - Leviticus 18:22
       b. Idols - Deuteronomy 7:25
       c. Involvement with the Zodiac, etc. - Deuteronomy 18:9-12
       d. Remarriage of divorcees who had after their divorce married others - Deuteronomy 24:4
       e. Use of unfair scales - Deuteronomy 25:16
       f. Wearing clothes that pertain to a man or vice-versa - Deuteronomy 22:5

    2. Notice, nowhere does it say pants or dresses. God is

interested in clear distinction. If culture and society changes to where the majority of women wear pants AND the majority of men wore dresses or robes, the Christian lifestyle would follow society. What you wear is not the main issue. Clear sexual distinction is the issue.
3. Society's recognition for the need for distinction is observed by the fact that restrooms are still symbolically marked as being for men or women. The symbol for a man shows him in pants. The symbol for a woman portrays her in a skirt.
4. Sexual distinction means that you can be denoted as male or female if I am looking at you from a distance.

I realize that much of the material covered today and over the past weeks is brand new to you. Living a holy lifestyle is a progressive thing. One does not become a mature Christian overnight, neither does one understand everything about the Bible and Christian living in a day. Your development depends on obedience. The things you receive are to be obeyed. Things received are those things taught and comprehended. The reasoning is understood. It is my observation that when a person decides to be disobedient in a particular area, it freezes his or her growth in all areas of Christian life. It is only when they decide to submit totally to God's will for their life that their Christian growth can continue.

Carlton L. Coon Sr. Bear Fruit – Teacher's Manual

Session Ten - Survey Sheet
"Specific Principles of Christian Living"

Name: _____ Date: _____

1. What does 1 Timothy 2:8-10 teach about the clothes we wear?

2. How is a Christian to be distinguished from those of the world? What does Simon Peter say should not be our distinguishing marks?

3. What are some things that are likely to happen when one dresses immodestly?

4. Give a single scripture reference where makeup is viewed in a positive fashion.

5. Based on what we have already learned, what is the difference between a Biblical principle and a personal conviction? Based on this, does the pastor have a right to set some standards or guidelines in the areas of modesty, jewelry, and makeup?

6. Why should we avoid "costly array?" Give a scriptural reference.

7. What two things does the Bible use to publicly identify us as either male or female?

8. What six reasons should a woman have long, uncut hair as she prays?

9. Why is Deuteronomy 22:5 relevant for this time?

10. Is there any portion of this lesson you would like to have dealt with in a more complete fashion.

Session Eleven
OVERCOMING TEMPTATION

Goal of This Lesson: To teach *how* temptation comes to us, and what we should do when temptation comes our way.

In the time you have been a Christian, there is little doubt that you have faced temptation. It is possible that you have even yielded to some temptation that has come your way. It is important to realize that you will never outgrow temptation. As long as you live for God, temptation will strive to destroy your walk with God. Think about it like this: If you are being tempted, Satan doesn't have you yet. If you are never tempted to do wrong, he probably already has you.

I. Discuss: What are some temptations that you will possibly face?

    A. Genesis 3:1-6 records the first temptation. Read these verses in conjunction with 1 John 2:15-16. Eve experienced:
        1. The (lust of the eyes). She saw the tree was good to look at.
        2. The (lust of the flesh). She perceived it to be good for food.
        3. The (pride of life). She knew it would make her wise.

    B. Read James 1:13. It is essential for us to realize that there is a difference between (trial) and (temptation).
        1. Discuss: Does God ever tempt us? What does tempt us?
        2. Discuss: Does God allow us to go through trials?
        3. Discuss: What are some trials that we may face?
        4. Discuss: What purpose do trials have?

    C. Read Matthew 7:24-27 - the parable of the two men who built on the rock and sand.
        1. What is the difference between the two men in this story?
        2. Why are people tempted by different things?
        3. Read James 1:13-15.
            a. God doesn't tempt us.
            b. Every man is tempted.
            c. Our lust (the word means "desires") is the basis of our temptation.
            d. Lust results in sin.

II. You Can Stand Above Temptation

    A. Job was able to. When he had lost everything and his wife encouraged him to curse God and die, he refused to do so.

B. The Spirit of the Lord will raise up a standard against Satan. (Isaiah 59:19)

C. Read 1 Peter 1:6.   Temptation precedes rejoicing.

D. Read Ephesians 6:13.   To overcome we need the whole armor of God.

E. Read 2 Peter 2:9.   God will deliver out of temptation.

F. Read 1 Corinthians 10:12-14.   Pride sets us up to be tempted.

III. How can we avoid temptation?

A. Read 1 Thessalonians 5:22.   Stay away from the appearance of evil.

B. Read James 4:7.   By submitting to God and resisting the devil.
1. Note that submission to God precedes resisting the devil.
2. Only in submission do we start resisting the devil.

C. Read Ephesians 6:10-18.   What six things make up the whole armor of God:
1. _____
2. _____
3. _____
4. _____
5. _____
6. _____

D. Practical Advice
1. Matthew 26:41   "Pray that we enter not into temptation."
2. 1 Thessalonians 5:22   "Stay away from anything that has the appearance or potential for evil."
3. What you look at opens the door to temptation.   Pornography, many romance novels, most movies, and soap operas open the door to wrong thoughts.   In computer terminology - Garbage In, Garbage Out!
4. Be careful of what happens when you're depressed or under pressure.   There are times when Satan will subtly send temptation your way.
5. Don't get too big for God to deal with you.

IV. What about when I sin?

      A. Read 1 John 2:1.
- 1. We are not to sin.
- 2. But if we sin, we have an advocate (spokesman, attorney) with the father.

      B. Read 1 John 1:9.

V. There are some sins that seem only to be conquerable by an individual becoming accountable to a mature Christian friend. Situations like repeated temptation to sexual misconduct, returning to addictive behaviors, and such can best be dealt with by confession and accountability. In accountability, the person battling temptation asks a mature Christian to help them be accountable on a regular basis. They agree on how often they will meet (generally monthly). They also agree on the questions that will be asked by the mature believer.

Carlton L. Coon Sr.   *Bear Fruit – Teacher's Manual*

Session Eleven - Survey Sheet
"Overcoming Temptation"

Name: _____ Date: _____

1. What does the word lust mean? (You may have to do some research for this answer.)

2. What is the difference between a trial and a temptation?

3. Why do you suppose the Bible informs us that God does not tempt us?

4. What do you do to avoid being tempted?

5. Write your thoughts about being accountable to someone. The Bible speaks of confessing our faults one to another. How does this relate to overcoming habits?

6. Is there any portion of this lesson you would like to have reviewed?

Additional copies of this book or other material by the same author may be ordered from:

CarltonCoonsr.com

Or

Carlton L. Coon Sr.

4521 North Farm Road 165

Springfield, MO   65803

To schedule a seminar on Disciple-making, Evangelism, Ministerial Development, Pastoral Development, Building Influence (Leadership) or Church Growth Systems

Email: carltoncoonsr@gmail.com

Phone: (314) 497-9801

Facebook: Carlton Coon Sr.

Twitter: @CarltonLCoonSr

Audio/Video of weekly preaching/teaching: SpringfieldCalvary.church

Materials Available:

(Prices Subject to Change)

Title	Price
New Convert Care - The How and Why!	$12
Follow Up Visitation - How and Why!	12
Hospitality – How and Why!	10
Take Root – Teacher's Manual (English or Spanish)	18
Take Root – Student (English or Spanish)	12
Bear Fruit – (Second Level of Discipleship Teaching) Teacher	18
Bear Fruit – Student	12
The Daily Things of Christian Living	16
Diary of Daily Things	12
Masterful Preaching – Restoring the Place of Good News Preaching	16
If Everybody Here Were Just Like Me (what kind of church would this church be)	16
You Wouldn't Want an Ostrich for Your Mama – Being a Disciple-making Church	16
Honey from a Strange Hive (A collection of funeral sermons for varied situations)	16
Healthy Church – Start Here!	16
Questions Pentecostal Preachers Ask	16
Fitly Framed – Helping People a Place to Serve	20

Made in the USA
Columbia, SC
23 July 2022